D1178890

Little Hands
STORY BIBLE

Carine Mackenzie

Little Hands Story Bible

Before you read what God has to say to you, pray that he will teach you from his Word as he has promised. Ask him to instruct you and teach you in the way that you should go. Ask him to show you how wonderful he is and how much you need him.

Copyright © 1998 Carine Mackenzie
ISBN 978-1-84550-435-9
This edition published in 2009 and reprinted in 2011

First published in 1998
with different illustrations
Paperback, ISBN 978-1-85792-697-8
Hardback, ISBN 978-1-85792-342-1

Christian Focus Publications
Geanies House, Fearn, Tain, Ross-shire, IV20 1TW,
Scotland, United Kingdom
www.christianfocus.com;
email: info@christianfocus.com

Cover design by Daniel van Straaten
Illustrations by Raffaella Cosco
Printed in China

Stories from the Old Testament

Stories from the New Testament

Stories from the Old Testament

God Made the World

God made the whole world from nothing. He said, 'Let there be light,' and light appeared.

He spoke again and water appeared. He spoke again and the land was made.

He made plants and trees, the sun, moon and stars, and the birds, fish and animals.

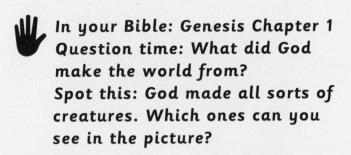

He made all this in six days. Everything that God made was very good.

In your Bible: Genesis Chapter 1
Question time: What did God make the world from?
Spot this: God made all sorts of creatures. Which ones can you see in the picture?

Give thanks to God for the beautiful world he has created.

God Made People

On the sixth day God also
made the first man. He was
called Adam. God made him
from the dust of the ground. God breathed
life into Adam and he became alive.

God did not want Adam to be alone so
he made a woman called Eve to be his wife.
God made Eve from one of Adam's ribs.

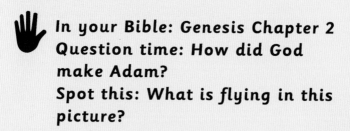

**In your Bible: Genesis Chapter 2
Question time: How did God
make Adam?
Spot this: What is flying in this
picture?**

**Give thanks to God for the person he
has created you to be.**

Garden of Eden

Adam and Eve lived in the
beautiful Garden of Eden.
There were lovely trees
there with good fruit to
eat.

Adam's job was to look after the garden.
He gave names to all the animals and birds.
God was their friend.

God allowed Adam and Eve to eat any of
the fruit in the garden except for one special
tree in the middle of the garden - the tree of
the knowledge of good and evil.

 **In your Bible: Genesis Chapter 2
Question time: What was
Adam's job?
Spot this: What colour are the
birds in this picture?**

**You can be like Adam and look after
God's plants and animals.**

Sin Spoils God's World

One day in the garden, Satan came, looking like a serpent and spoke to Eve, 'Did God really say you should not eat the fruit of the special tree?'

'Yes,' said Eve. 'If we do we will die.'

'That's not true,' said Satan.

Eve believed Satan. She took some of the fruit and gave some to Adam too. They both sinned by disobeying God. They were sent away from the garden as a punishment.

 In your Bible: Genesis Chapter 3
Question time: What did Adam and Eve do wrong?
Spot this: What animal is on the tree?

We should obey God and not listen to the devil.

Noah Builds the Ark

People in the world were very bad. God decided to send a flood to destroy all the wicked people. He warned good Noah and told him to build a big boat for himself, his wife and his three sons and their wives.

They did what God told them and built the ark of wood, with a window and a door. The ark had three decks - plenty of room for Noah and his family and at least two of every animal.

 In your Bible: Genesis Chapter 6 and 7
Question time: Why did God send a flood?
Spot this: Where are the ladybirds?

> **You can be like Noah and do something special for God.**

Rainbow Promise

Noah and his family were kept safe in the ark until the rain had stopped and the flood water had gone back down again. God told Noah to come out of the ark with his wife and family and all the animals.

God made a beautiful rainbow in the sky, as a sign of his promise, never to flood the whole earth again.

 In your Bible: Genesis Chapter 8 and 9
Question time: What promise did God make to Noah?
Spot this: What is Noah holding in his hand?

You can be like Noah and his family and trust God.

Abraham

Abraham and his wife, Sarah, lived in a land far away. God spoke to Abraham and told him to go on a long journey to another country. God promised to look after him. Abraham did as God asked.

God promised to bless him and his children. A baby boy called Isaac was born when Abraham and Sarah were very old. God kept his promise to them.

In your Bible: Genesis Chapters 12–21

Question time: What was the name of Abraham and Sarah's baby boy?

Spot this: How many people are in this picture?

You can be like Abraham and do what God asks you to do.

A Wife for Isaac

Abraham's servant was sent
back to his home country to
find a wife for Isaac. He made
the long journey with ten camels.

He went to the well at evening time when
the young women came to get water. The
servant asked one young woman to give him
a drink.

This kind girl gave the servant a drink at
once and also brought water for his camels.
The girl was called Rebekah. She went back
with the servant to become Isaac's wife.

 **In your Bible: Genesis Chapter 24
Question time: What was Isaac's
wife called?
Spot this: How many camels can
you see in the picture?**

You can be like Rebekah and be kind
and helpful to others.

The Twins

Isaac and Rebekah had twin sons called
Jacob and Esau. Sometimes twins look
very like each other. Jacob and Esau were
completely different.

   Esau was red and his skin was hairy.
Jacob's skin was smooth.

   Esau loved hunting wild
animals out in the country
while Jacob liked to stay
near home.

 **In your Bible: Genesis 25: 1-34
Question time: Which twin
loved hunting?
Spot this: What is Jacob holding
in this picture?**

**God made us all different and he
loves each of us very much.**

Joseph's Special Coat

Joseph had eleven brothers, but his father loved him best. His father gave him a lovely coat with many beautiful colours. His brothers were upset.

Joseph had two dreams. The meaning of the dreams was that Joseph would be more important than his brothers. The brothers disliked him all the more.

 In your Bible: Genesis 37: 1-11
Question time: Why did the brothers not like Joseph?
Spot this: How many sheep can you see in the picture?

God does not want us to be upset when others receive something good.

Joseph Goes to Egypt

One day Joseph's father sent him to find out how his brothers were. They were in the country looking after the sheep. When they saw him coming they made a plan to get rid of him. They put Joseph in a deep pit.

When some travellers came along, they sold Joseph as a slave for twenty pieces of silver. He was sent to Egypt. The boys then tricked their father, to make him believe Joseph was dead.

 In your Bible: Genesis 37: 12-36
Question time: How much was Joseph sold for?
Spot this: How many coins is the man holding in his hand?

God does not want us to be nasty to our brothers and sisters.

Joseph Helps his Brothers

God helped Joseph through all his hard times. He was a slave and had to work very hard. Then he was thrown into prison – a wicked woman told lies about him. God was still with him.

Because Joseph told the king the meaning of a dream, he was given an important job looking after the grain crops. Many years later, men from a far off land came to buy food from Jospeh. They were his brothers.

 In your Bible: Genesis Chapters 39–45
Question time: Who helped Joseph all the time?
Spot this: What colours can you see in Joseph's clothing?

God promises to be with us even when life is hard and things go wrong.

Baby in the Basket

Pharaoh, King of Egypt, was cruel. He hated God's people and wanted all the baby boys killed. One mother and father bravely made a plan to save their baby. They made a basket of rushes and placed the baby inside. As it floated in the river, it was watched by his big sister.

The baby was found by the princess who kept him for her own son, but she asked the mother to be his nurse. She called him Moses.

 In your Bible: Exodus Chapters 1–2
Question time: How was the baby kept safe?
Spot this: What creatures can you see in the water?

> God promises to look after us, even when we are very young.

The Burning Bush

Moses was looking after the sheep in the desert. He saw a bush on fire, but the bush did not burn up. How strange! Moses went nearer to see better.

God spoke to him from the bush. 'Do not come any closer. Take off your shoes. You are standing on holy ground.' Moses was afraid. 'I am sending you to rescue my people from slavery,' said God. 'I will be with you.'

 **In your Bible: Exodus 3: 1-14
Question time: What was Moses told to take off?
Spot this: Where are Moses' shoes?**

God promises to be with us especially when we are afraid.

The Red Sea

The people of Israel left the land of Egypt where they had been slaves. Moses was their leader, helped by his brother, Aaron. God showed them where to go.

A pillar of cloud led them in the day and a pillar of fire at night. When they came to the Red Sea, God caused the sea to part and a dry road was made for them right through the sea. The people of Israel left the land of Egypt where they had been slaves. Moses was their leader. Everyone crossed safely.

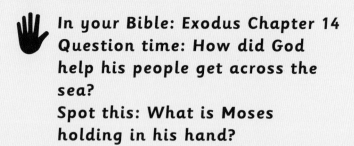

In your Bible: Exodus Chapter 14
Question time: How did God help his people get across the sea?
Spot this: What is Moses holding in his hand?

God promises to lead us safely wherever he calls us to go.

Manna

God gave food to the people as they travelled across the desert. Every morning God covered the ground with small white seeds called 'manna'.

The people collected this, crushed it and then made cakes with it. The people gathered just enough for that day. On the day before the Sabbath they were given enough for two days.

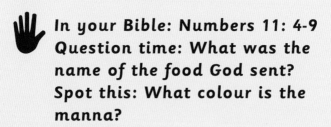

In your Bible: Numbers 11: 4-9
Question time: What was the name of the food God sent?
Spot this: What colour is the manna?

God wants us to give thanks for our daily food.

Water from the Rock

There was no water in the desert
and the people were thirsty.
They grumbled to Moses and
Aaron. Moses and Aaron prayed
to God. God said to Moses,
'Gather the people together. Speak to
that rock and water will pour out of it.'

All the people came to Moses. He
hit the rock twice with his stick. Water
poured out. All the people and the
animals had enough to drink.

 In your Bible: Numbers 20: 1-13
Question time: How did Moses get
water from the rock?
Spot this: What animal can you
see in this picture?

God does not want us to grumble
about things, but to trust him.

38

The Ten Commands

God called Moses to the top of Mount Sinai. He gave him ten commandments for the people to follow. The commands were written on two big stones by God.

Jesus summed up the commands like this - you should love God with all your heart, soul, strength and mind. You should love your neighbour as yourself. We should obey these commandments too.

In your Bible: Exodus 20: 1-17
Question time: Who did Jesus tell us to love?
Spot this: How many stones is Moses holding in this picture?

God wants us to obey his commandments.

Joshua

Joshua and the people
marched on to Jericho. The
walls were high. The gates were tightly shut.
But God was with them. He told them what to
do. 'March round Jericho for six days.'

Round and round they marched, with
the priests blowing their trumpets. On the
seventh day they marched round seven times.
Everyone shouted loudly. The big strong
walls fell down flat. Joshua and the people of
Israel had won the battle of Jericho. God had
helped them.

**In your Bible: Joshua 6: 1-20
Question time: How did the
walls fall down?
Spot this: What is Joshua
leaning his hands on in the
picture?**

God wants to help us win our battles.

Gideon

Gideon had lots of
soldiers in his army.
'Your army is too big.' said God, 'you think
you do not need my help.'

Lots of men decided to go home. 'Your
army is still too big. Tell the men to take a
drink from the river.'

The men who took the water up to their
mouths with their hands were the ones who
were chosen. Gideon and his small army won
the battle with God's help.

 **In your Bible: Judges Chapter 7
Question time: Who helped
Gideon win the battle?
Spot this: How many men are
drinking from the river?**

**We cannot win our battles without
God's help.**

Ruth and Naomi

Ruth's mother-in-law, Naomi, wanted to go back to her homeland – to Bethlehem. Both women were widows; their husbands had died.

Ruth decided to go with Naomi. 'Do not ask me to leave you,' she said. 'I want to go where you go. Your people will be my people and your God will be my God.' How glad Naomi would be to have Ruth with her.

In your Bible: Ruth Chapter 1
Question time: Where was Naomi's home town?
Spot this: What does Ruth have on her arm?

You can be like Ruth and ask God to be your God.

Ruth and Boaz

Ruth went out to the fields to gather up any grain that the workers had dropped. She went to Boaz's field.

Boaz was very kind to her. 'Drop some grain on purpose,' he told his workers, 'so that Ruth can gather plenty to take home to Naomi.

Naomi was so pleased when Ruth came home with a large amount of grain.

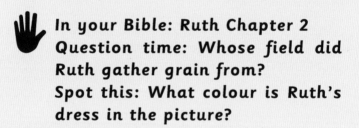

**In your Bible: Ruth Chapter 2
Question time: Whose field did Ruth gather grain from?
Spot this: What colour is Ruth's dress in the picture?**

You can be like Ruth and help your relatives and family.

Birth of Samuel

Hannah was very sad because she did not have any children. She wanted to have a baby very much. She went to the House of God and prayed that God would give her a baby boy. God answered her prayer.

Some time later she had a baby boy of her own. She called him Samuel, which means, 'asked of God', because she had prayed to God for this baby boy.

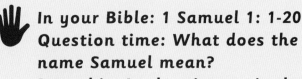

In your Bible: 1 Samuel 1: 1-20
Question time: What does the name Samuel mean?
Spot this: In the picture, is the baby awake or asleep?

You can be like Hannah and trust God will answer your prayers.

God calls Samuel

One night Samuel was lying in bed in the temple. He heard a voice calling his name, 'Samuel.'

'Here I am,' he called back running through to Eli.

'I did not call you,' Eli replied. 'Go back to bed.'

After hearing the voice three times, Samuel knew that it was God speaking to him. 'Speak Lord for your servant is listening,' he said. God spoke to Samuel.

 In your Bible: 1 Samuel Chapter 3
Question time: What did Samuel say to God?
Spot this: Can you point to the lamp in the picture?

> **You can be like Samuel and respond to God in prayer.**

David the Shepherd

David was a shepherd boy who looked after his father's sheep. He worked out on the hillside taking the sheep to find food and water. He was very brave.

Once a lion and a bear came to steal a lamb. David caught them both and rescued the lamb. God looked after David and kept him safe.

In your Bible: 1 Samuel 17: 34-36
Question time: Who looked after David?
Spot this: What is David looking after in this picture?

God promises to look after you just as he did with David.

David the Fighter

Goliath was a wicked giant who fought against the people of Israel. 'I will fight against Goliath' said young David. 'God will help me.'

He took five smooth stones and his shepherd's sling and faced up to the big giant.

David aimed one stone which hit Goliath right in the forehead. He fell down dead. David had saved his people from the enemy.

 In your Bible: 1 Samuel Chapter 17
Question Time: What did David use to fight Goliath?
Spot this: What is Goliath holding?

God promises to help us fight the giant problems in our lives.

Queen of Sheba

The Queen of Sheba heard
how wise King Solomon
was. She wanted to find out for herself if
this was really true. She travelled a great
distance to Solomon's palace. She arrived
with camels carrying gifts - spices, gold and
jewels.

She asked Solomon lots of hard questions
and he answered them all. Nothing was too
hard for him to explain.

When she went home, she knew that
Solomon was very wise.

**In your Bible: 1 Kings 10: 1-13
Question time: What animals
did the Queen of Sheba arrive
with?
Spot this: What does the Queen
of Sheba have in her hands?**

**You can be like the Queen of Sheba and
bring your gifts to God.**

Fed by the Birds

For a long time there was no rain, which meant that the crops could not grow. Elijah, the man of God, was hungry and thirsty. God told him where to go to get a drink from a little river. So Elijah had water to drink.

'I have told some birds called ravens to bring food for you,' God told Elijah. The ravens brought bread and meat to Elijah, every morning and every evening.

 In your Bible: 1 Kings 17: 1-7
Question time: Who brought food to Elijah?
Spot this: How many birds can you see in this picture?

God will always provide our food if we trust in him.

Plenty to Eat

A mother went out to gather sticks to make a fire. There was hardly any food in the land. She was going to make some bread with her last drop of oil and flour, when she met Elijah, the man of God.

'Bake me a cake first,' he said.

'God will provide enough for you and your boy.'

The jar of oil did not run dry and the bin of flour was not used up. The lady, her son and Elijah had plenty to eat.

 In your Bible: 1 Kings 17: 8-16
Question time: What did the lady use to make the bread?
Spot this: How many bowls can you see on the rock?

You can trust God for your food even when there seems to be nothing to eat.

Naaman

Naaman was a brave
soldier, but he had
a horrible disease,
called leprosy. The little servant girl said
to Naaman's wife, 'If only my master could
see the man of God in my home country, he
would make him better.'

Naaman went to see Elisha, the man
of God. He told him to wash in the River
Jordan. His leprosy was cured. How happy
the little servant girl must have been.

In your Bible: 2 Kings 5: 1-15
**Question time: What was wrong
with Naaman?**
**Spot this: What can you see on
the river bank?**

**You can be like Naaman and trust God
to make you well.**

Nehemiah Builds the Walls

The walls of Jerusalem had been broken down. Nehemiah was sad to hear this. He asked his master, the King of Persia, if he could go back to build up the walls again. The king said, 'Yes.'

What a huge task for Nehemiah! Many people made fun of him and even tried to stop the work. But God helped Nehemiah. The wall was finished in only fifty two days.

 In your Bible: Nehemiah Chapters 1–6
Question time: What did Nehemiah build with God's help?
Spot this: What is the man with the beard carrying?

You can be like Nehemiah and trust God even when people laugh at you.

The Lions' Den

Daniel loved God. He prayed to him often. Some bad men did not like Daniel. They made the King make a bad law - anyone who prayed to God was to be put into a den of lions.

Daniel prayed as usual. He was put into the lions' den. But God kept him safe, the lions did not hurt him.

In your Bible: Daniel Chapter 6
Question time: Who kept Daniel safe in the lions' den?
Spot this: How many lions can you see in the picture?

You can be like Daniel and trust God when in danger.

Jonah Runs Away

God told Jonah to go to a city far away to tell people about him. Jonah was afraid and sailed away in a boat. A big storm came. The other sailors threw Jonah into the sea, but he did not drown. God sent a large whale to swallow Jonah.

Jonah was put out by the whale on dry land. Then he did what God had asked him to do.

 In your Bible: Jonah Chapters 1–4
Question time: How did Jonah reach dry land?
Spot this: Can you find Jonah in this picture?

You can trust God and not be afraid when he tells you to do something.

Stories from the
New Testament

The Birth of Jesus

One day an angel came to visit Mary. 'You are going to have a very special baby,' he told her. 'Do not be afraid. You shall call his name Jesus.' Mary was amazed at this news. How could that happen?

'Your baby is the Son of God,' said the angel.

Mary's baby was born while she was visiting Bethlehem. There was no room in the inn. The special baby was born in a stable and laid to sleep in a manger.

 In your Bible: Luke Chapters 1–2
Question time: Why was Mary afraid?
Spot this: How many cakes are in the bowl in the picture?

You can give thanks to God for sending Jesus into the world as a baby.

Shepherds in the Fields

Some shepherds were out in the fields one night taking care of their sheep. An angel came to them with great news. 'Today in the town of Bethlehem the Saviour has been born.'

The shepherds hurried to Bethlehem and found baby Jesus lying in a manger. The shepherds praised God for the birth of this baby. They told the good news to everyone they met.

In your Bible: Luke 2: 8-20
Question time: In which town was Jesus born?
Spot this: How many sheep are in the picture?

You can be like the shepherds and tell others about Jesus.

The Wise Men

Wise men from an eastern country came to look for Jesus. They had seen a special star in the sky.

They wanted to meet the new king that had been born. They followed the star. It led them to where Jesus was. They brought lovely presents for the baby — gold and incense and myrrh. They bowed down and worshipped Jesus.

 **In your Bible: Matthew 2: 1-12
Question time: Who were the wise men looking for?
Spot this: What colour is the wise man's beard?**

You can bring the gift of yourself to Jesus.

Jesus Grows Up

Jesus grew up in the town of Nazareth with his family.

Joseph was a carpenter who made things from wood. Jesus' mother was called Mary. He had several brothers and sisters.

Jesus grew strong and healthy and wise. He was like no other child. He did not do anything wrong.
He always did
what God wanted
him to do.

In your Bible: Luke 2: 39-40
Question time: What was Joseph's work?
Spot this: What does Joseph have in his hand?

You can ask Jesus to help you to be good.

Jesus in Jerusalem

When Jesus was twelve years old, he went with his parents to Jerusalem for a special feast.

Crowds came from all over the country. On the way home Mary and Joseph realised that Jesus was missing. They rushed back to Jerusalem to look for him. At last they found Jesus in the temple, speaking with the wise teachers.

'Did you not know that I had to be in my Father's house,' he said. He was meaning God, his Father.

 In your Bible: Luke 2: 41-52
Question time: Where did Mary and Joseph find Jesus?
Spot this: How many sheep can you see in the picture?

You can learn about God and Jesus by reading the Bible.

Simple Peter

Simon was a fisherman
on the Sea of Galilee.
One day his brother,
Andrew, told him good news about Jesus.
'He is the one sent by God to take away the
sins of the world,' said Andrew.

Andrew took his brother, Simon, to
meet Jesus. Jesus asked Simon and Andrew
to follow him and be among his twelve
disciples. Jesus gave Simon a new name –
he called him Peter.

**In your Bible: John 1: 35-42
Question time: Who took Simon
to meet Jesus?
Spot this: How many fish can
you see in the picture?**

You can be like Andrew and Simon Peter
and follow Jesus.

The Wedding

Jesus and his mother and his friends were guests at a wedding. In the middle of the party, Jesus' mother came to him and said, 'They have no more wine.' She was sure he could help.

Jesus told the servants to fill up six big pots with water. Jesus then turned the water into the very best wine.

✋ **In your Bible: John 2: 1-11
Question time: Who turned the water into wine?
Spot this: What kinds of fruit can you see?**

You can be like Mary and trust Jesus to help you when faced with problems.

Wise and Foolish Builders

Jesus told a story about two men who were building a house. The wise man built his house on a rock. It was firm and strong. When the rain and winds came, the house was safe.

   The foolish man built his house on sand. When the rain and wind came, his house came crashing down and was washed away. 'The wise person listens to God's Word and lives by it,' Jesus said.

 In your Bible: Matthew 7: 24-27
Question time: Whose house stood firm?
Spot this: How many palm trees can you see in this picture?

You can be like the wise man by listening to God's Word and living by it.

Four Good Friends

A poor, lame man lay on his mat all day long. He couldn't walk. He had four good friends. 'Let's take our friend to Jesus,' they said. So they carried him on his mat to the house where Jesus was, but because of the crowds of people, they could not get in.

They climbed up the outside stair, opened up the roof and lowered their friend down in front of Jesus. 'Your sins are forgiven,' said Jesus. 'Take your mat and go home.' The man was cured.

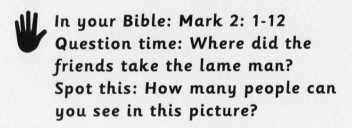

**In your Bible: Mark 2: 1-12
Question time: Where did the friends take the lame man?
Spot this: How many people can you see in this picture?**

You can be like the four friends and bring someone to Jesus.

The Farmer

Jesus told a story about a farmer sowing the seed. Some seed fell on the path and birds ate it up. Some fell on the rocky ground and it soon died. Some fell among the thorns and the plant soon died.

But some fell on good ground and it grew well and gave a good harvest. If we listen to Jesus' words and obey them, that is like the good seed.

 In your Bible: Matthew 13: 1-9 Question time: What happened to the seed that fell on the path? Spot this: How many birds can you see in the picture?

You can be like the good seed by listening to and obeying Jesus' words.

The Sick Boy

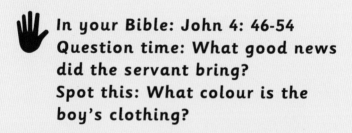

An important man from
Capernaum had a little boy who
was very sick. 'Please come to see my son
before he dies,' the father begged Jesus.

'Your son will live,' Jesus replied. 'Go back
home.'

The father believed Jesus. Before he
reached home, his servant came running
to meet him. 'Your son is better.' He had
got better at the exact time that Jesus had
spoken to his father.

In your Bible: John 4: 46-54
Question time: What good news
did the servant bring?
Spot this: What colour is the
boy's clothing?

You can be like the father and believe
God will answer prayer.

Pool of Bethesda

Around the pool of Bethesda were many people who could not see or walk.

One lame man had been there for a long, long time. He had no friend to help him.

'Do you want to get better?' asked Jesus. 'Get up, pick up your mat and walk.' At once the man was better. He picked up his mat and walked off.

In your Bible: John 5: 1-9
Question time: Who made the lame man better?
Spot this: How many people can you see in this picture?

You can pray to God. Jesus wants you to be well.

Calming the Storm

Jesus and his friends went out in a boat across the lake of Galilee. Jesus fell asleep. A storm suddenly blew up and waves swept over the boat. The friends were afraid and woke Jesus. He got up and spoke to the wind and the waves.

'Quiet! Be still!' At once, all was calm. His friends were so amazed by Jesus' power.

In your Bible: Mark 4: 35-41
Question time: How did Jesus calm the waves?
Spot this: Is the water calm or stormy in the picture?

You can pray and ask Jesus to calm the storms in your life.

Jesus Loves Children

Jesus loves little children. Little children were brought by their parents to Jesus so that he would put his hand on them and pray for them.

The disciples tried to turn them away but Jesus said, 'Let the little children come to me. Don't stop them. The kingdom of heaven belongs to them and those like them.'

**In your Bible: Matthew 19: 13-15
Question time: Was Jesus pleased to see little children?
Spot this: How many children are in the picture?**

Jesus always has time for you even when you are young.

Jairus' Daughter

Jairus' little girl was very ill. Jairus went to find Jesus to ask him to make her well. By the time Jesus came to her house the little girl had died.

Jesus went into her room with her mother and father and his friends John, James and Peter. He said to the little girl - 'get up!' She sat up in bed. Jesus had made her better. 'Give her something to eat,' Jesus said.

In your Bible: Luke 8: 40-56
Question time: What did Jesus say to the little girl?
Spot this: What is the little girl doing in the picture?

Jesus always has time for you even when you are ill.

The Kind Man

A poor man lay badly hurt on a lonely road. He had been robbed and beaten up. One man came along, but he hurried past. Then another man came; he looked but hurried on too.

Then a kind man came along on his donkey. He felt so sorry for the poor man. He bandaged his wounds, then put him on his donkey and took him to an inn where he looked after him. Jesus tells us to be like the kind man.

In your Bible: Luke 10: 25-37
Question time: What did the kind man do?
Spot this: What is on the poor man's head in the picture?

Jesus wants us to be like the kind man.

Mary and Martha

Mary and Martha were sisters who were friends of Jesus. Jesus would often go to their house for a meal.

One day Martha was busy cooking, while Mary sat listening to Jesus. Martha complained to Jesus. 'Why is Mary leaving me to do all the work?'

'Don't be so worried about serving the supper,' said Jesus. 'Mary is right to spend the time listening to me.'

In your Bible: Luke 10: 38-42
Question time: Which sister loved to sit and listen to Jesus?
Spot this: How many bowls can you see in the picture?

Jesus wants us to be like Mary and spend time listening to him.

Lazarus

Mary and Martha's brother, Lazarus, became very sick. The sisters sent for Jesus, but before he came, Lazarus died. Mary and Martha were very upset. When Jesus arrived, he was very sad too. He asked to be taken to where Lazarus was buried.

'Take away the stone,' he said to their amazement. 'Lazarus come out!' he called.

By the wonderful power of Jesus, the Son of God, Lazarus was alive again!

In your Bible: John 11: 1-44
Question time: Who were Lazarus' sisters?
Spot this: Are Mary and Martha happy or sad in this picture?

We can believe that Jesus will help us when we are upset.

Jesus Feeds the Crowd

Out in the country one day crowds of people were listening to Jesus. By evening they were hungry, but there was no food or shops nearby. Only one little boy had a picnic with him - five small loaves and two small fish.

Jesus said thank you to God for the food and his friends gave it out to the people. Because of Jesus' power everyone had enough. There were even twelve baskets left over!

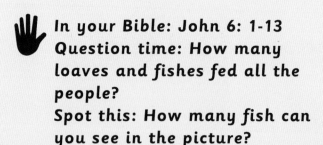

In your Bible: John 6: 1-13
Question time: How many loaves and fishes fed all the people?
Spot this: How many fish can you see in the picture?

You can be like Jesus and always give thanks for your food.

The Woman who was Made Better

One Sabbath, Jesus was teaching in the church. A lady came in who could not even stand up straight. Her back was bent over.

She had suffered for a long time. Jesus called out to her, 'You are free from your problem.' He touched her and at once she could stand up straight.
How she praised God!

In your Bible: Luke 13: 10-17
Question time: What did the lady do when she was cured?
Spot this: What colour is the lady's dress?

You can believe that Jesus will set you free from your problem.

The Loving Father

Jesus told a story about a young man who left home. He wanted to have a good time. When his money ran out, all his friends left him. He had no food and no place to stay.

'It would be better if I were just a servant in my father's house,' he thought. 'I will go home.'

His father saw him coming from a long way off. He ran out to meet him and welcomed him home again.

In your Bible: Luke 15: 11-32
Question time: How did the father show his son how much he loved him?
Spot this: What colour is the father's clothing?

God forgives those who say sorry for their sin and come back to him.

The Lost Sheep

Jesus told this story to show how much he loves and cares for even one person.

A man had one hundred sheep. One day a sheep got lost. The man left all the other sheep safely grazing and went to look for the lost one. He was so happy when he found it. He had a party with his friends to celebrate.

In your Bible: Luke 15: 1-7
Question time: How many sheep did the man have?
Spot this: Where is the sheep caught in the picture?

Jesus loves you very much and will take care of you.

The Lost Coin

Jesus told the story of a
woman who had ten precious
silver coins. One day one of
the coins was lost. She lit the
lamp, took her brush and swept
every corner of the house. At last she found
the missing coin. How pleased she was. She
shouted to her friends, 'I have found my lost
coin.' They were very happy for her.

Jesus wants us to know that the angels in
heaven are so happy when one lost sinner is
found by him.

 In your Bible: Luke 15: 8-10
Question time: How many coins
did the lady have?
Spot this: Where is the lost coin
in the picture?

Jesus is so happy when you come to
him and say sorry for your sin.

The One who Gave Thanks

One day Jesus met ten men on the road. They all were very ill with a bad skin disease. 'Jesus, please make us better,' they called. As they walked along the road they were cured.

One of them, when he saw he was healed, came back to Jesus to thank him. He praised God as loudly as he could. 'What about the other men?' Jesus asked. Only one came to say thank you.

In your Bible: Luke 17: 11-19
Question time: How many were healed?
Spot this: What is on the man's arms and feet in the picture?

We should always thank Jesus when he does something wonderful for us.

Zacchaeus

Nobody liked Zacchaeus, the tax collector
- he was a cheat. One day Jesus came to
town. Zacchaeus wanted to see him but he
was so small he could not see Jesus over the
crowd. He climbed a tree to get a good view.
Jesus noticed him and said, 'Come down. I
want to come to your house today.'

Zacchaeus was so pleased. 'I will pay back
all the money I have taken by cheating,' he
said. What a difference meeting Jesus made
to Zacchaeus.

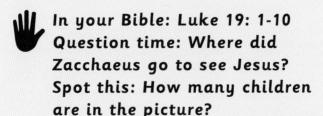 **In your Bible: Luke 19: 1-10
Question time: Where did
Zacchaeus go to see Jesus?
Spot this: How many children
are in the picture?**

**We should ask Jesus to help us to be
honest in all we do.**

Children in the Temple

Jesus rode into Jerusalem on a donkey. Crowds of people were shouting, 'Hosanna in the Highest.'

When he reached the temple, he healed blind and lame people. The children gathered round and shouted praise to Jesus. 'Hosanna to the Son of David.' Jesus was pleased to hear the children praise him.

In your Bible: Matthew 21: 12-16
Question time: What did the children shout out?
Spot this: What are the people holding in their hands in the picture?

We too can sing our praises to Jesus for all he has done.

On the Cross

Jesus was cruelly treated. All his friends left him.
He was taken to a place called Calvary and nailed to a cross of wood. There he died.

Why did this happen? Not just because wicked men hated Jesus. God must punish sin. Jesus took the punishment himself, so that boys and girls who love and trust him can have all their sins forgiven.

 In your Bible: Luke 23: 26-49
Question time: Where did Jesus die?
Spot this: Can you point to Jesus' cross in the picture?

We can come to Jesus and ask him to forgive our sins.

Empty Tomb

Jesus' body was buried in a tomb. A big stone was put at the entrance. Some ladies came early in the morning to see where he had been buried. They found the big stone had been rolled away. Jesus' body was not there! Two angels told them the good news. 'He is not here; he has risen.'

The ladies rushed to tell this good news to Jesus' friends.

In your Bible: Luke 24: 1-12
Question time: Who told the ladies the good news that Jesus had risen?
Spot this: How many ladies are there in the picture?

We can tell our friends that Jesus is alive today.

On the Shore

Peter and six friends went out
to fish but caught nothing.
A man called out to them from the shore,
'Friends, have you any fish?'
　'No' they said.
　'Throw out your net on the right side of
the boat.'
　When they did that they caught many
fish. One friend realised that the man was
Jesus. Peter jumped out of the boat and
rushed up the shore to greet him. They all
had bread and fish for breakfast.

In your Bible: John 21: 1-14
Question time: What did they
have for breakfast?
Spot this: Who is jumping into
the water in the picture?

**We can run to Jesus and tell him that
we love him.**

The Lame Man

One afternoon Peter and John went to the temple to pray. A lame man sat at the gate begging. He asked Peter and John for money.

Peter said, 'I have no silver or gold, but I will give you something else. Rise up and walk!'

He pulled the man to his feet. The man could now walk for the first time. He went into the temple jumping for joy and praising God.

 **In your Bible: Acts 3: 1-10
Question time: What did the man do after he was healed?
Spot this: In this picture, what does the man have in his hand?**

You can be like the man who was healed by praising God for all his goodness.

Damascas Road

Paul went to Damascus, meaning to harm the Christians who lived there. On the road a bright light from heaven flashed round him, blinding him. He fell to the ground. The Lord Jesus spoke to him.

Paul was led into the town. Ananias was sent to help him. Scales fell from Paul's eyes and he could see again. Paul's life was changed. He loved the Lord Jesus now.

In your Bible: Acts 9: 1-19
Question time: What happened to Paul on the road?
Spot this: How many horses are there in the picture?

You will have joy in your heart when you turn from your sin to Jesus.

Dorcas

Dorcas was good at
sewing. She made
clothes for poor
families. The mothers
and children loved her.

Dorcas became ill
and died. Her friends were so upset. They
sent for Peter and begged him to help.

Peter went to Dorcas' room and prayed to
God. 'Get up!' he said. She opened her eyes
at once. Her friends were so happy.

 In your Bible: Acts 9: 36-43
**Question time: What happened
to Dorcas?**
**Spot this: What colour is the
tunic Dorcas is making in the
picture?**

**You can be like Dorcas and help those
who are poor and needy.**

Escape from Prison

Peter was put in prison because he was a Christian. His Christian friends prayed for him.

One night an angel came and woke Peter up. 'Get up quickly,' he said. The chains fell off Peter's hands. He followed the angel out to the street, then he went to the house where his friends were praying.

They got such a surprise to see Peter safely out of prison. What an answer to their prayers!

In your Bible: Acts 12: 1-19
Question time: How did Peter get out of prison?
Spot this: What colour is Peter's tunic?

God loves to hear us pray to him.

Lydia

Lydia was a very busy person. Her work was to sell purple cloth. She loved to go to the riverside to pray with the other women.

One day she heard Paul preaching there, about the Lord Jesus.

She decided to follow Jesus and wanted to do all she could for him. She asked Paul and his friends to stay at her house.

 In your Bible: Acts 16: 11-15
Question time: Where did Lydia go to pray?
Spot this: What colour is Lydia's head covering?

You can be like Lydia and follow the Lord Jesus.

Paul the Preacher

Paul preached the good news about Jesus in many places. He was very brave. He was even put in prison, but God sent an earthquake to shake the prison. The prison guard asked Paul, 'What must I do to be saved?'

Paul gave him the only answer, 'Believe in the Lord Jesus and you will be saved.' The prison guard was very happy.

In your Bible: Acts 16: 25-34
Question time: What did Paul tell the guard to do?
Spot this: How many people are in this picture?

You can be like Paul and tell other people about the Lord Jesus.

Timothy

Timothy learned parts of the Bible when he was just a young boy. His mother and his grandmother taught him the ways of God. They both loved and trusted God and Timothy learned to do the same.

He became a missionary when he grew up and travelled with his friend, Paul - telling people in other lands about the Lord Jesus Christ.

 In your Bible: Acts 16: 1-5 and 1 and 2 Timothy.
Question time: Who taught Timothy about the ways of God?
Spot this: What colour is Timothy's hair in the picture?

You can be like Timothy and learn the Bible while you are young.

CHRISTIAN FOCUS PUBLICATIONS

Christian Focus · Christian Heritage · CF4K · Mentor

Christian Focus Publications publishes books for adults and children under its four main imprints: Christian Focus, CF4K, Mentor and Christian Heritage. Our books reflect that God's word is reliable and Jesus is the way to know him, and live for ever with him.

Our children's publication list includes a Sunday School curriculum that covers pre-school to early teens; puzzle and activity books. We also publish personal and family devotional titles, biographies and inspirational stories that children will love.

If you are looking for quality Bible teaching for children then we have an excellent range of Bible story and age specific theological books.

From pre-school to teenage fiction, we have it covered!

Find us at our web page:
www.christianfocus.com

CF4•K
Because you're never too young to know Jesus